D1709593

CHEVROLET CORVETTE Z06

BY CALVIN CRUZ

BELLWETHER MEDIA • MINNEAPOLIS, MN

Are you ready to take it to the extreme? Torque books thrust you into the action-packed world of sports, vehicles, mystery, and adventure. These books may include dirt, smoke, fire, and dangerous stunts.
WARNING: read at your own risk.

This edition first published in 2016 by Bellwether Media, Inc.

Library of Congress Cataloging-in-Publication Data

Cruz, Calvin, author.
Chevrolet Corvette Z06 / by Calvin Cruz.
pages cm -- (Torque. Car crazy)
Summary: "Engaging images accompany information about the Chevrolet Corvette Z06. The combination of high-interest subject matter and light text is intended for students in grades 3 through 7"--Provided by publisher.
Includes bibliographical references and index.
Audience: Ages 7-12.
Audience: Grades 3-7.
ISBN 978-1-62617-280-7 (hardcover : alk. paper)
1. Corvette automobile--Juvenile literature. I. Title.
TL215.C6C78 2016
629.222'2--dc23
2015007536

Printed in the United States of America, North Mankato, MN.

TABLE OF CONTENTS

A NEW RECORD

A crowd gathers at a racetrack. A Chevrolet Corvette Z06 pulls up to the starting line. The driver wants to test the speed of his new **supercar**.

He sees the signal and pushes the pedal to the floor. The engine roars as the Z06 **accelerates** down the track.

The Z06 is soon traveling almost 200 miles (322 kilometers) per hour! The crowd watches the Z06 fly past in a flash. Then the car comes to a stop. The Z06 has run the quarter-mile in under 11 seconds!

THE HISTORY OF CHEVROLET

In 1911, a Swiss race car driver and the American who started General Motors had an idea. Louis Chevrolet and William C. Durant wanted to make cars that were comfortable and performed well.

Louis Chevrolet

William C. Durant

A DARING DRIVER

LOUIS CHEVROLET SET A LAND SPEED RECORD IN 1905. HE DROVE 111 MILES (179 KILOMETERS) PER HOUR!

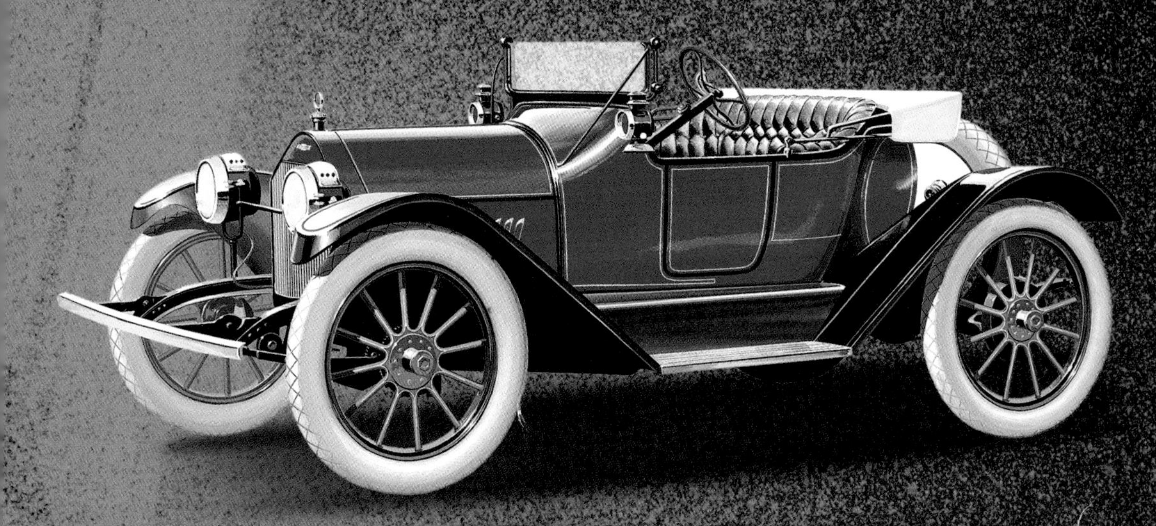

1914 Chevrolet Royal Mail Roadster

Many people knew the Chevrolet name from Louis's racing success. The two men named the company after Louis to help sell the cars. They also priced the cars lower than similar cars made by other companies. Their cars were a hit!

General Motors bought the Chevrolet name in 1917. Chevrolet continued to design popular cars with a low cost. It also started making more expensive cars. In 1953, Chevrolet showed off the first Corvette at the New York Auto Show.

Today, Chevrolet makes cars that perform well across all price ranges. It is one of the world's biggest car companies!

1953 Chevrolet Corvette

1953 New York Auto Show

CHEVROLET CORVETTE Z06

The Z06 is a more powerful version of the Corvette **model**. The first Z06 came out in 1963. This car was designed for the racetrack. Since then, the Z06 has gone through three **generations**. The newest Z06 generation began in 2015. It is made by the same team that designs Chevrolet race cars.

1963 Chevrolet Corvette Z06

2015 Chevrolet Corvette Z06

TECHNOLOGY AND GEAR

The Corvette Z06 is made to be light yet powerful. It can come as a **coupe** or a **convertible**. The coupe's hood and roof are made of **carbon fiber**. The convertible has a soft top. In nice weather, the convertible's roof can be removed!

The car's frame and engine are made of **aluminum**. The engine has a **supercharger** to give it more power.

coupe

convertible

LT4 supercharged
V8 engine

spoiler

The Z06 is **aerodynamic**. It sits low to the ground to cut through the wind. The wide body allows for larger tires. Its body shape and **spoiler** help the tires grip the road at high speeds.

The Corvette Z06 has many features to make driving easier. Drivers can add **paddle shifters** on the steering wheel to change gears.

For different driving conditions, the Z06 has five settings to help the car perform its best. With the turn of a dial, the driver can change the car's **handling** and power.

paddle shifters

RACE REVIEW

A RECORDER IN THE Z06 LETS DRIVERS SEE THEIR TOP SPEEDS AND ENGINE PERFORMANCE AFTER THEY FINISH THEIR DRIVE.

2015 CHEVROLET CORVETTE Z06 SPECIFICATIONS

CAR STYLE	COUPE OR CONVERTIBLE
ENGINE	6.2L LT4 SUPERCHARGED V8 ENGINE
TOP SPEED	ABOUT 200 MILES (322 KILOMETERS) PER HOUR
0 - 60 TIME	ABOUT 3.0 SECONDS
HORSEPOWER	650 HP (485 KILOWATTS) @ 6400 RPM
CURB WEIGHT (COUPE)	3,524 POUNDS (1,598 KILOGRAMS)
(CONVERTIBLE)	3,582 POUNDS (1,625 KILOGRAMS)
WIDTH	77.4 INCHES (197 CENTIMETERS)
LENGTH	177.9 INCHES (452 CENTIMETERS)
HEIGHT	48.6 INCHES (123 CENTIMETERS)
WHEEL SIZE	19 INCHES (48 CENTIMETERS) FRONT 20 INCHES (51 CENTIMETERS) REAR
COST	STARTS AT $79,000

TODAY AND THE FUTURE

The Corvette Z06 is the most powerful sports car ever made by Chevrolet. Drivers love the look, feel, and power of the supercar. Owners like having a car they can drive on the streets and the track. The Corvette Z06 will continue to blur the line between race car and supercar!

FLEX YOUR MUSCLES

THE TELEVISION SHOW *TOP GEAR* NAMED THE Z06 ITS MUSCLE CAR OF THE YEAR FOR 2014.

HOW TO SPOT A CORVETTE Z06

LARGE AIR VENTS

SPOILER

WIDE FENDERS

GLOSSARY

accelerates—increases in speed

aerodynamic—having a shape that can move through air quickly

aluminum—a strong, lightweight metal

carbon fiber—a strong, lightweight material made from woven pieces of carbon

convertible—a car with a folding or soft roof

coupe—a car with a hard roof and two doors

generations—versions of the same model

handling—how a car performs around turns

model—a specific kind of car

paddle shifters—paddles on the steering wheel of a car that allow a driver to change gears

spoiler—a part on the back of a car that helps the car grip the road

supercar—an expensive and high-performing sports car

supercharger—a part that increases an engine's power

TO LEARN MORE

AT THE LIBRARY

Kenney, Karen Latchana. *Thrilling Sports Cars.* North Mankato, Minn.: Capstone Press, 2015.

Quinlan, Julia J. *Corvette.* New York, N.Y.: PowerKids Press, 2013.

Von Finn, Denny. *Super Cars.* Minneapolis, Minn.: Bellwether Media, 2010.

ON THE WEB

Learning more about the Chevrolet Corvette Z06 is as easy as 1, 2, 3.

WWW.FACTSURFER.COM

1. Go to www.factsurfer.com.

2. Enter "Chevrolet Corvette Z06" into the search box.

3. Click the "Surf" button and you will see a list of related web sites.

With factsurfer.com, finding more information is just a click away.

INDEX

The images in this book are reproduced through the courtesy of: Jim West/ Glow Images, front cover; General Motors, pp. 4-5, 6-7, 8-9, 10-11, 12-13, 14-15, 16-17, 18-19, 20-21.